Farmhouses and Manors of Long Island

AMERICANA

SCHIFFER
PUBLISHING

4880 Lower Valley Road • Atglen, PA 19310

Kyle Marshall

Edited by Cheryl Weber
Art direction by Jacqueline Anerella
Designed by Danielle D. Farmer
Cover design by Danielle D. Farmer
Type set in GT America Black / Baskerville Old Face / Avenir

ISBN: 978-0-7643-5786-2
Printed in China

Published by Schiffer Publishing, Ltd.
4880 Lower Valley Road
Atglen, PA 19310
Phone: (610) 593-1777; Fax: (610) 593-2002
E-mail: Info@schifferbooks.com
Web: www.schifferbooks.com

For our complete selection of fine books on this and related subjects, please visit our website at www.schifferbooks.com. You may also write for a free catalog.

Schiffer Publishing's titles are available at special discounts for bulk purchases for sales promotions or premiums. Special editions, including personalized covers, corporate imprints, and excerpts, can be created in large quantities for special needs. For more information, contact the publisher.

We are always looking for people to write books on new and related subjects. If you have an idea for a book, please contact us at proposals@schifferbooks.com.

For my grandmother, Joan

DO THE HUSTLE

Albertson-Meyer House, Oyster Bay

CONTENTS

FOREWORD

I have been asked to write a foreword to this book, even though I'm acquainted with the subject only peripherally. My wife, Mary Abbene, and I own what she refers to as a collection of shacks—not altogether ironically. Our business, a design studio specializing in letterpress printing and engraving, occupies two adjacent buildings cobbled together as temporary structures in 1899—with no foundations or any other allegiance to commonly accepted engineering principles. We live in a house similarly situated, formed as an irregular pearl around a single room from 1660 and added onto layer upon iridescent layer to form a luminous whole. All three of our shacks reflect the nature of things that accrete organically, that adapt to the vagaries of circumstance by necessity, and that have incorporated prevailing sensibilities over successive moments in time.

I first encountered Kyle Marshall at our shop, when he came in one Saturday to order business cards—and I took note of his selection. It brought to mind a book I'd read years ago, *The Common Sense of Yacht Design*, by L. Francis Herreshoff, and one anecdote in particular. Working for his father at the Herreshoff shipbuilding yard, the author recalled that each prospective new hire—draftsman, jointer, machinist, rigger, painter, et al.—was asked to make a box. There were no specifications accompanying that directive—no size, shape, or method of construction. As a result, the person under consideration was left entirely to their own devices, and the box they produced was a preeminent reflection of how they approached the proposition—their ability to translate an idea into actuality, their technical proficiencies and aesthetic judgment, and how they balanced all the factors against practicality. When I saw the design of Kyle's business cards, this story lingered with me.

A couple of years later, I bumped into him on Instagram and was captivated by his photos and the words that accompanied them. And so, while the box he had built in the form of a business card had hinted at his sensibilities, his postings revealed him more fully, with more depth and texture and resonating clarity.

So it came to pass—with a certain inevitability—that I encountered Kyle at a benefit for Raynham Hall, a historic house museum here in Oyster Bay. As I mentioned, I live in an old house and had come across some odd-looking bricks when working on one of the many projects that come with all old houses. They were about the same length as modern bricks but wider and more squat, more irregular, and pockmarked with a multitude of imperfections. In talking with Kyle at the benefit—our first conversation of any real substance and duration—I'm sure I came across as a wild-eyed crazy, what with my bubbling-over enthusiasms for my bricks in particular and my house in general.

The thing is, however, those bricks are truly fascinating and tell their own story. As Nabokov wrote in *Transparent Things*, "when we concentrate on a material object, whatever its situation, the very act of attention may lead to our involuntarily sinking into the history of that object." Thus it was clear to me that at some point in the very distant past, a person now long forgotten had fabricated a small frame of wood, plopped it on the ground, filled it with a slurry of clay, and screed the surface off with their hand—because here were the striations and contours left by a palm sweeping across the top . . . and on the underside was the impress of blades of grass so clear they could be counted. As I blathered on, with Kyle asking questions and inserting his own two cents (and no sideways glances for the exit), I could tell I'd met a kindred spirit.

According to Horace, a picture is a poem (*ut pictura poesis*), inasmuch as it tells a story. Kyle's book on a subject heretofore relegated to obscurity tells the many stories of Long Island farmhouses and manor houses vividly and compellingly. Though his focus employs the long lens of looking back, this is no dry recitation of dates and places, nor a reveling in the dewy-eyed nostalgia of bygone times. Rather, it's a collection of vignettes and musings, and through this exercise he demonstrates, with verve and vibrancy, how the past is always present—that far from being dusty artifacts, these places remain as buoyant and alive today as they were in yesteryear.

WILLIAM MILLER
Co-owner
The Printery
Oyster Bay, New York

Youngs Farmhouse, Old Brookville

Youngs Farm, Old Brookville

The Homestead, Nissequogue

INTRODUCTION

I. Between Sound and Sea

My earliest memories are the scents of a childhood near Long Island Sound, of sweet honeysuckle and beach rose, pungent low tide, and wet dirt roads. As a teenager I worked as a carpenter's go-for on the North Shore, exposed to the diversity of Long Island farmhouses. Later, while a student at Rhode Island School of Design, I came to see these houses as multigenerational examples of *gesamtkunstwerk*–total works of art. Situated in beautiful surroundings, their evolution is humbling and astounding.

I hope this book satiates those who hunger for old houses. Our appetite is a longing for atmosphere, and this book is about the atmospheres in and around Long Island farmhouses, a type of vernacular building found on this singular island, the largest of the Outer Islands. Each is a medley of history, architecture, furnishings, memories of people, and the tidal ebb of our current lives. It is not so much survey as banquet, a sequence of excellent examples that do not demarcate the limits of the subject but suggest the many variants that exist or have existed or might, through influence, appear in the future.

Certain of these houses are small, and others are big; some are sweet and some almost savory. But all are many layered. The delight they offer is not accidental but the result of centuries of building and stewardship on an island set between the sound and the sea.

II. Americana

Building is at its best when it is an effort to tell a story–often grounded both in fact and fiction–about inhabitants and their communities. Though buildings are often interpreted as expressions of function, logic and necessity alone do not rule the human spirit. Rather, it is in the pursuit of beauty that houses are often made, remade, and remodeled.

We look at the world's abundance of housing for architectural and historical ideas to reference, new stories to weave into our own. A house is an ongoing story, and no house can become a home without furnishings and people in its midst. In the case of the houses of Long Island revealed here, the atmospheres of their interiors and exteriors are as I found them in the first quarter of the twenty-first century. They embody centuries of ownership and building activity, an aesthetic evolution shaped both by Dutch and English colonial origins, and proximity to the cultural crossroads of Long Island Sound and New York City. Each has faithfully anchored successive generations engaged in the art of living amid evolving American taste, each generation expanding, altering, and redefining these houses as dictated by popular trends and personal, often-esoteric passions. The growth and evolution of these buildings, their inspiring architecture and current charmed interiors, reflect both broad American trends and also uniquely local influences.

Long Island's unusual histories–a former Algonquin tributary land, the location of the first New World manor granted to a woman, the home of America's first published slave poet, a wellspring of twentieth-century colonial revival design fervor–are reflected in its singular buildings, long prized as ideal country retreats by American poets, writers, artists, and designers. Both William Floyd, a signer of the Declaration of Independence, and Anna Wintour, editor in chief of *Vogue*, have fallen under the spell of their own Long Island farmhouses. These houses and their interiors, connected to history and animated by eccentricity, represent a maverick Americana.

The deepest influence on Long Island farmhouses has been the island itself, which sustained Algonquin communities for 5,000 years before Europeans arrived in the seventeenth century. The island's length revealed a variety of distinct habitats to the new arrivals: enormous salt meadows along creeks and bays; vast beaches of white sand along the South Shore's barrier islands; freshwater wetlands; noble pine barrens; deciduous forests; majestic, treeless prairie land; undulating downs; freshwater bogs, ponds, streams and rivers; and finally the North Shore necks of woodland and pebbled beach. These habitats and those of the island's dependent islands (Robins, Shelter, Plum, Gardiners, and the South Shore barrier islands, including Long Beach and Fire) were stripped of their resources as Europeans imported old conflicts to the New World. Ongoing power struggles among and with the Algonquins forged a century of immense, often-harrowing change for everyone, including the island: its vast natural resources were extracted as increasing numbers of Europeans arrived. Television today often rightly depicts an eighteenth-century land denuded of its magnificent trees. A constant, then and now, has been the surrounding waters, which range in scale from intimate creeks and coves to grander bays and the magnificent sound and, of course, the mighty Atlantic, all waterways that connect the island with communities near and remote.

New York City's emergence during the nineteenth century as a cultural capital saw many Long Island houses—their myriad charms wrapped in the region's notable long wood shingles—embraced by connoisseurs. They continue to bring to these houses a romantic spirit, embracing the warm scent of wood floorboards, sunlight washing over plaster walls, and crisply painted sash windows of old, wavy glass. These often-rambling houses easily absorb the alternating peace and chaos of daily life.

Americana is a porous word. Like the country itself, it permits a number of disparate, even conflicting cultural elements to shelter beneath the same roof. It is unpretentious, for it absorbs camp lore and kitsch mid-twentieth-century signage as easily as fine eighteenth-century antiques. This unique quality, which often seems a nostalgic contradiction to the prejudiced eye, is in fact an elegant art that weaves together the serious and the frivolous—that is to say, the dominant strands of the human condition. Long Island farmhouses, unique to the island, are likewise repositories of building, decorating, farming, and gardening, forms of dwelling given dignity through human hands, places of our labor and love. The practical evolutionary growth of these houses—an extra wing here, another porch there, interiors confidently arranged and enveloped by history, all situated with ease in the landscape—feels quintessentially, confidently American.

III. Evolutionary Building

Architecturally, Long Island farmhouses descend from Dutch and English building techniques and styles. The seventeenth-century houses initially erected by the Dutch on the western end of the island and by the English on the eastern end followed their respective homeland precedents. These early wood-frame houses were generally one or two rooms in plan with an end chimney stack. Through sequential additions they evolved into the recognizable Dutch colonial of the island's western end and the Cape Cod and lean-to styles of the eastern end. Between these separate building traditions there exists a wide region where the two practices merged. The island's middle band, situated between present-day Brooklyn and the beginning of the north and south forks, contains the bulk of these houses. Many began as one or two rooms that grew through a series of additions, usually extended laterally, with wings flanking a near-symmetrical main block, and, in the most-complex examples, longitudinal rear wings. Others began as high-style eighteenth-century houses and saw their greatest additions during the post–Civil War period, when new affluence recast them as summer retreats.

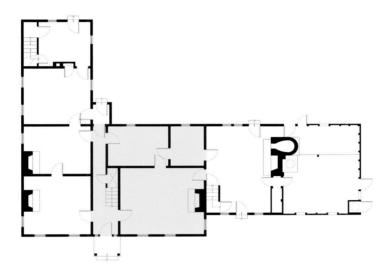

Plan I. Powell Farmhouse, Old Bethpage
The pink area highlights the footprint of the original house, ca. 1750. Several stages of expansion resulted in the current dimensions, ca. 1870. Plan drawn by Sanjay Kumar Verma on the basis of drawings included in a 1969 report by John R. Stevens, supervising architectural historian of Architectural Heritage, consultants to Old Bethpage.

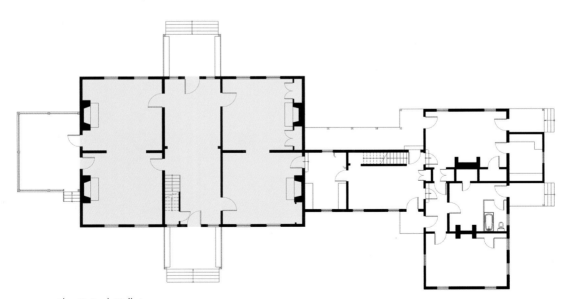

Plan II. Rock Hall, Lawrence
The pink area highlights the footprint of the original house, ca. 1767, later remodeled in the Federal style ca. 1790. The service wing dates to 1881; formerly, services were accommodated in separate buildings. The large side porch no longer exists. Plan drawn by Sanjay Kumar Verma on the basis of drawings of the Historic American Buildings Survey (HABS).

Long Island farmhouses of the middle-band region grew along several lines during the colonial and federal periods. They originated as either seventeenth- or eighteenth-century homestead houses, such as Powell Farmhouse, Old Bethpage (plan 1), or provincially grand eighteenth-century houses such as Rock Hall, Lawrence (plan 2). Both types were extended by craftsmen over time as their families' needs evolved. Many homesteads grew by the addition of a side-hall wing three bays wide (two windows and a door), which gave the entire assemblage a more architecturally sophisticated air. The original house would often be treated as a kitchen wing, with the addition containing two proper reception rooms and a genteel stair hall mediating between the old and new construction.

In Oyster Bay, which is the dividing line between the seventeenth-century Dutch and English power spheres, William Miller and Mary Abbene's Albertson-Meyer house is a marvelous example of a later side-hall addition to a Dutch-influenced homestead. Standing in lush gardens screened from the world by majestic yews, the house is a sarabande sequence of accretive building. The original Dutch-style house (ca. 1660s), with its projecting eaves and massive open hearth, was expanded west at the end of the seventeenth century, the low profile maintained. The late eighteenth century witnessed the addition of the side-hall wing, still the westernmost wing of the house, with later twentieth-century additions focused on expanding eastward from the kitchen. A two-story summer sleeping porch breathes air into the whole.

Other side-hall-addition houses were further, more intensely remodeled to achieve the beaux ideal of a five-bay-wide, symmetrical block, with two more bays added to the side-hall addition in order to compose the grander, desired whole. Owing to stair layout and the fact that the addition was often not quite a mirror image of the existing side hall, these five-bay-wide blocks were in fact asymmetrical. A third story with bands of frieze windows (sometimes referred to as eyebrow windows) was frequently added, to express a fashionable, vaguely Greek Revival sensibility, as well as to unify the not-quite-symmetrical façade below that had grown across several generations. Charming Hay Fever (chapter 8) is an excellent example of the type.

The eighteenth-century high-style houses—the most architecturally sophisticated and built in connection with a plantation economy, such as Rock Hall (chapter 5) and Sylvester Manor (chapter 14)—saw remodeling but little growth to their building envelopes until after the Civil War, when several assumed the role of summer country houses. Functions previously accommodated in ancillary buildings, such as cooking and washing, were brought into the main house via additional wings.

This tradition of aggregate building occurred in all three regions of the island, influencing new houses constructed at the beginning of the nineteenth century, such as Casa Blanca (chapter 12), and existing-home renovations. The architecturally conservative earlier houses influenced the builders of new houses, who integrated national forms of architecture, such as the Federal style, in subtle rather than overt ways. Old Mastic (plan 3), the in situ jewel of the Fire Island National Seashore, demonstrates accretive growth and a façade that harmonized over time to encompass urbane notions of architecture—epitomized by the symmetrical main block—along with the more practical concerns accommodated by rambling north wings: one long and thin, with a narrow summer kitchen with bedrooms and sleeping porches above; the other a winter kitchen with spacious service facilities.

There are exceptions to subtlety, including Raynham Hall of Oyster Bay. Built ca. 1738 as a center-chimney house, it was immediately extended through the north to assume the air of a classic saltbox. A century later it was remodeled by architect Edward H. Thorne for the Townsend family in the

Albertson-Meyer House, Oyster Bay

Plan III. Old Mastic, Mastic
The pink area highlights the footprint of the original house, ca. 1729. The lateral span was relatively complete and included matching wings, ca. 1791. The western wing was later removed. The northeast wing predates the northwest wing (added ca. 1897). Plan drawn by Sanjay Kumar Verma on the basis of drawings in the Historic American Buildings Survey (HABS) report.

fashionable Gothic Revival style. He removed the central chimney to make way for a cupola, and the façade was encrusted with porches, French doors, and projecting bay windows—a Gothic dolls' house complete with many gables and a tower porte-cochere. This reconfiguration by a practicing architect rather than craftsmen predates that of many Long Island farmhouses. Raynham Hall's current appearance, a street façade of serious colonial revival clapboard and a playful Victorian garden wing, owes as much to earlier building traditions as to a mid-twentieth-century interpretation of its historical character.

IV. Long Island Farmhouses in the Twentieth Century

By the nineteenth century, Long Island farmhouses were undeniably part of a local building tradition, exhibiting a range of influences. These charming houses, with just enough ramble to raise curiosity, were and are a visible presence along lanes and waterways. Their heritage proved particularly alluring for colonial revivalists, who saw houses ripe for reinvention within a reasonable distance from New York City.

The city's explosive growth during the nineteenth century introduced to Long Island a new group of aesthetes, connoisseurs, antiquarians, collectors, and architects in search of old houses to reinvent as their country retreats. This Long Island Revival co-opted existing farmhouses, and some former manor houses—all pieced together over the prior quarter millennium—for use as atmospheric places of repose.

The Long Island Revival was heavily influenced by the Colonial Revival movement, which erupted after the Philadelphia Exposition of 1876. Another influence was Long Island's parallel Gold Coast epoch, whose gilded excess served as a foil for the intentional understatement sought by those seeking old farmhouses to imbue with new, rosier life. Stanford White, of the architectural firm McKim, Mead & White, bridged the gap between these two aesthetics. In 1884 he married Bessie Smith of St. James, a member of that prominent North Shore family whose coffers had been conveniently refreshed through inheritance. The family was thus in the unusual position of being locals who toyed with fashionable architecture. White purchased a relatively unremarkable nineteenth-century farmhouse, renamed it Box Hill, and began a decades-long renovation that would allow him to explore his ideas about harmonizing disparate decorative elements. The pebble-dashed house with many gables, surrounded by a good helping of ancillary buildings, was more than a glorified farm group; it was a miniature Gold Coast estate, a gentleman's farm created in an ersatz American vernacular, one not particularly native to Long Island.

White would go on to renovate a number of local houses associated with his wife's family, including Bessie's sister's estate, Sherrewogue. White gave the seventeenth-century house, with multiple later additions, a thorough colonial-reveal renovation—more of the original Long Island than he had bequeathed to Box Hill.

Later architects, influenced by an increasingly serious attitude toward early American vernacular building, also sought out older houses already embedded in the landscape. Architects prone to eclecticism in their work seemed particularly drawn to Long Island's old farmhouses, which evinced a gradual building evolution. William Lawrence Bottomley, best known for designing Colonial Revival country houses along the Eastern Seaboard and for his extensive townhouse designs in

Richmond, Virginia, bought Hickory Hill, built ca. 1680s, in Old Brookville in 1924. One of Long Island's oldest houses, saltbox in massing, it was refreshed with Colonial Revival dormers and a general program of renovation, but its intrinsic fabric—old paneling, large fireplaces, and immense original front door—were preserved. The residence of a gentleperson, its heritage was glazed rather than painted over.

Between the years of White's freestyling colonial efforts and Bottomley's reverent aesthetic, there were firms working on the island whose architects referenced specific Long Island building and aesthetic traditions. Of these, it is Peabody, Wilson & Brown, a firm noted for its fluency working in a variety of architectural idioms, from Neo-Georgian at Land of Clover, Nissequogue, to the modernist The Shallows, Southampton, that was the most masterful and perhaps prolific in charting the twentieth-century course of Long Island farmhouses. Numerous renovation commissions across the North Shore bear their understated stamp—an ability to harmonize the existing building fabric with new notions of domestic architecture and practical conveniences, much as Norman Jewson did in the Cotswolds. The firm's presence on the island may be attributed to its high-society partner Archibald Brown; it was for his brother Lathrop that they designed Land of Clover. In 1910, Brown himself purchased East Farm, a ca. 1710 house in Head of the Harbor, and spent the next two decades reinventing it as a modern saltwater gentleman's farm (plan 4). He added a vast dining room whose massing was balanced by the addition of a service wing, the whole circulation reoriented around a new stair hall between the old house and the new additions. East Farm balanced a desire for grandeur with the perception of simplicity. Its appearance, however, remained unabashedly that of a shingle-clad Long Island farmhouse, its lateral growth exaggerated through Brown's additional rambling roofline.

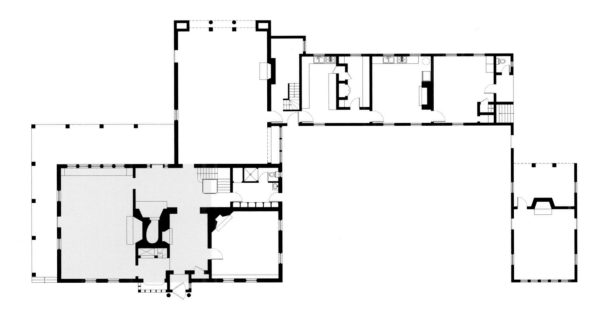

Plan IV. East Farm, Head of the Harbor
The pink area highlights the author's estimated footprint of the original house and its early expansion, ca. 1710–50. Later expanded by Archibald Brown of Peabody, Wilson & Brown in 1910. Plan drawn by Sanjay Kumar Verma on the basis of drawings submitted to *Architectural Record*, July–December 1915.

Many of these architectized houses were published, advertising a Long Island overrun by picturesque farmhouses surrounded by blooming apple orchards near saltwater bays. Long Island Revival was never presented explicitly as such; it was instead featured as a blissful ideal for sophisticated rather than homespun retreat. *House & Garden's* 1911 Long Island Supplement compressed history, land speculation, and real estate into what we might now call sponsored content, a narrative of old houses with the scope to accommodate modern people. It touched on the fantasy of small-scale farming balanced against practical commuting concerns.

The photographic record shows reverence for the historical nature of the comfortably decorated rooms, without their owners' appearing formal. Rather, we visualize them walking barefoot through the houses, their casual regard denoting their familiarity with such surroundings. Over time, Long Island became known for its understated rambling-yet-unostentatious farmhouses. Among the many examples, a 1973 article in *Vogue* chronicled the photographer Toni Frissell Bacon's life in bare feet and pearls; she enjoyed life outdoors as much as inside at Sherrewogue, which she purchased with her husband, Francis. The house was portrayed as a series of covered porches sheltering endless potted plants, interiors decorated by water views as much as by quilted chintz. Like many others, the Bacons carried on the tradition of stewardship of a house and its land.

Other houses attracted the attention of connoisseurs and creative people with lives centered on New York City. Some, such as the antiquarian and Preservation Long Island founder Howard C. Sherman, used the island and its old houses to explore the colonial period. Sherman purchased the eighteenth-century Sherwood-Jayne Farm, Setauket, in 1908. He commissioned architect Joseph Everett Chandler to extend and restore the main house, preserving its eighteenth-century wall frescoes and incorporating salvaged elements, such as paneling, from local houses. Chandler and Sherman approached the process with creative flair, masking their additions as historical when in fact their interpretation was wholly in keeping with the evolution of these homes, ongoing experiments in American building and material culture.

The use of salvaged colonial-era materials, a hallmark of twentieth-century historicism, was also undertaken by Henry Davis Sleeper, known for his epic life's work, Beauport, a many-roomed house of artistic experiment in Gloucester, Massachusetts. Sleeper freely used salvaged paneling and architectural details in his pursuit of a fantasy interior, sheathing newly built rooms in historical paneling while channeling a twentieth-century vision of the past.

Sleeper's free-spirited understanding of American material culture inspired Henry Francis du Pont, founder of Winterthur. Sleeper advised du Pont on an extension to Winterthur, which today sprawls in the same manner as Beauport. After Sleeper's death, du Pont turned toward Bertha Benkard for advice on his collection. Benkard, owner of Horton House, Old Brookville, Long Island, was known for her expertise in Phyfe furniture and approached furniture and interiors in a more rigorous, period-specific manner. At her Long Island farmhouse she realized her particular vision of American antiques within the atmospheric envelope of a country house. Her sitting room, composed of paneling from the Smith-Nichols House, Newburyport, Massachusetts, included smart early Federal-period furniture and late-eighteenth-century silver, Chinese black lacquer nesting tables, and a painting of the naval battle fought off Sandy Hook in 1815. This room, paneling and all, was bequeathed in its entirety to the Metropolitan Museum of Art, expanding the museum's Federal-era holdings as well as its record of connoisseurship during the first half of the twentieth century.

Some individuals bequeathed whole houses and their contents to the public. Sagtikos Manor (page 45) and Old Mastic (page 145) are two delightful examples, the former a free-spirited interpretation of a historical interior by its last owner, the latter still imbued with a summer house atmosphere through layers of furniture and textiles cherished by generations. Others, such as Raynham Hall (this page) and Rock Hall (page 73), have been furnished, interpreted, and preserved by their respective communities.

Plan V. Foxland (Sayrelands), Bridgehampton The pink area highlights the footprint of the original house, ca. 1734. The caretaker's wing (*lower left*) dates from the third quarter of the twentieth century. Plan drawn by Sanjay Kumar Verma on the basis of drawings in the Historic American Buildings Survey (HABS) report.

Raynham Hall, Oyster Bay. The Victorian wing appears charmingly conjoined with the colonial portion on the right, reconfigured during the mid-twentieth century.

V. Today

I began creating this book after we bought our small farmhouse in Locust Valley several years ago. An early-nineteenth-century house, with a companion hayloft barn across the garden, it is one of many inheritors of the island's accretive building traditions.

Many other homes continue to be well loved. The sporting Concagh family's beloved Foxland, Bridgehampton (plan 5), a precious example of a Georgian-influenced Long Island farmhouse, envelopes all who enter its exceptional rooms. Their lives are surrounded by the beauty of exuberant eighteenth-century frescoes and paneling painted their chosen shades of vibrant robin's-egg blue and cardinal red. The Concaghs serve as remarkably informed stewards of the house, supremely comfortable in their august surroundings. The same can be said for the owners of the Homestead (page 23), Willow Hill (page 37), Turbillon (page 57), Thatch Meadow Farm (page 95), Hay Fever (page 107), Carhart House (page 133), Casa Blanca (page 159), Point Place (page 169), and the Terry-Mulford House (page 195).

Still other houses have been saved by virtue of their land. The Carl J. Schmidlapp House, Mill Neck, perhaps the most inventive of Peabody, Wilson & Brown's renovation commissions, sits on land recently saved by the North Shore Land Alliance, an organization that along with the Peconic Land Trust has done much to preserve the unique qualities of our island's landscape. The house itself, now surrounded by preserved land, awaits restoration by its new owners. Its Janus façades are incomparably charming: its southern façade is low key, elevated by a relatively humble two-story entrance porch, whereas facing north it is a prodigious Colonial Revival affair with an expanse of many shuttered windows.

Others continue to function as the domestic centerpiece of farming operations in family hands. The farmhouse of Youngs Farm, a locus of North Shore identity, has for 200 years watched over the rolling terrain, its evolution ongoing, and its most recent additions have been overseen by John Collins, one of the island's seminal architects. Now run by the fifth generation of the family, descended from Reverend John H. Youngs, who landed at Southold in 1642, the farm is an anchor for the entire community. Beautifully appointed with delicious arrangements of food, the farmstand is a reminder of the earthy yet refined pleasures of life on this unique and verdant island.

KYLE MARSHALL
East Village, New York City
May 2018

Our house on the day of purchase

View south from the **Carl J. Schmidlapp House**, Mill Neck. Landscape preserved through the North Shore Land Alliance.

THE HOMESTEAD
Nissequogue

The most satisfying approach to the Homestead is the same as it was hundreds of years ago: over the glistening currents of the sound, into Smithtown Bay, and onward across the clear, black-bottomed waters of Stony Brook Harbor. Here the horizon is all shoreline, with twin encircling ribbons of chartreuse saltwater grasses and green tree canopies separated by pebbled beach. Lackadaisical birds linger in the air, and tiny minnows school below.

Completing the tableaux at the end of the seventeenth century were wood-clad houses surrounded by clearings. At that time, perched on the western shore far from the mouth of the harbor, stood a little house with its back to a quiet hill. Its site formed part of a large area of land purchased in the 1660s by Richard Smith from Lion Gardiner of Gardiners Island, who had received the land from Sachem Wyandanch several years prior.

Thirty years later, in 1725, you would find a busier bay, with that small house just a bit more sophisticated. Ebenezer Smith grafted an addition onto the original house, which became a subsidiary wing. The larger new section presented a neat three-bay façade with two full stories. It was an example of architectural progression in this burgeoning community, whose homes still lacked flourishes such as dormers and welcoming porches. Within a few decades the main section was again expanded to a full five-bay length, bookended by the original chimney stack and a new eastern chimney.

During the nineteenth century, notes of casual ease crept in. A wraparound porch upended the simplicity of the exterior, running across the main five-bay section. It provided a wonderful place to take in the view, to be sure, but it was an ungainly addition for such a tightly conceived building. All else remained substantially the same, and the house stayed in Smith family hands until the beginning of the twentieth century, when it was purchased by William Dixon.

Dixon sought a smart Long Island farmhouse, an early-twentieth-century idealization of the island's colonial-era homestead houses favoring gentility and economy in equal measure—a stark contrast to the Gold Coast epoch that was winding down just as Dixon arrived. He commissioned Peabody, Wilson & Brown to discreetly insert modern conveniences and light Colonial Revival flourishes. The involvement of practicing architects, rather than talented builders or gentleman-designers, was a fairly new phenomenon on the island.

The house's existing simplicity and atmosphere guided the architects, who sympathetically adjusted the interior, preserving much of the dining-room paneling while creating a new eastern sitting room out of two smaller spaces. A new porch along the eastern depth of the house was sited to take in the morning light just above the beach below. The unusual staircase in the central hall, its rail supported by a single beveled panel rather than balusters, was retained for its solid charm rather than obliterated in favor of a lighter arrangement.

The exterior received a full Colonial Revival touch-up. Graphic shutters, paneled on the first floor and louvered on the second, introduced a sense of hierarchy to the overall massing and emphasized the dominance of the eighteenth-century section of the house. The shutterless older wing is an appendage that visually terminates in the adjacent pump house. Both sections acquired fashionable and practical dormer windows, lifting the perceived height of the façade, its rhythm further modulated by simple trim.

Today, the more usual approach to the Homestead, now back in Smith family hands, is by land. A long road runs through a dense woods, heightening the moment when a small rise opens up to fields and lawn that cascade down to the beach and bay beyond. The graveled lane rolls down this landscape and passes a scattered village of barns, garages, and stables before quickly ending in front of the house.

Traipsing across the gravel, you are drawn into the house—through the front door, through the stair hall—and just as quickly you are pulled out—through the garden door at the other end of the hall. A perfect small lawn, partially enclosed by boxwood, provides a sheltered spot to take in the astonishing view of the shimmering bay that laps at the pebbled beach below. Inevitably, the house lures you back inside, its unaffected interiors an amalgam of patterned wallpapers and colonial paneling, simple furniture, and tasteful rugs. It all adds up to an aesthetic balm. Everything feels settled; a sense of ease pervades the whole.

WILLOW HILL
Springs

Restraint and simplicity are the hallmarks of sophistication. Often confused with luxury or the absence of decorative effect, these virtues mark the paradoxical grandeur of humility. This middle-path philosophy dovetails neatly with rescuing the beau ideal of an old house, one untouched by the fashions of the immediately preceding decades. It takes a rare marriage of self-awareness and vision to guide an untouched atmosphere into the present day, a balance between the need to accommodate the present without eradicating the patina of the past. Willow Hill is a demonstration of excellence, where the architecture and atmosphere of the past are seamlessly grafted onto the present.

Peter Bickford and Greg McCarthy longed to rehabilitate a house innocent of messy twentieth-century intrusions, and when, during a bicycle ride, they came across Willow Hill, inhabited for decades by the same tenant, they had found a house to savor.

Willow Hill, its first portion built during the early eighteenth century, is idyllically situated south of the great salt hay meadows of Accabonac Harbor and originally formed the nucleus of a small homestead. Perhaps the finest example of a central-chimney farmhouse in the Springs, it reveals a clever, thoughtful evolution throughout the eighteenth to the end of the nineteenth century, the southern portion expanded during the former, and a perfect, minute kitchen wing added during the latter. When first constructed, it was undoubtedly a conservative building, a small house with its chimney stack on one side. Later, the stack was surrounded by rooms during a period of expansion to create a balanced three-bay facade.

Inside, the furnishings lend a self-assured feeling, with antiques casually placed about a series of rooms that are remarkably airy despite their cozy dimensions, in part because of well-placed windows. Bickford and McCarthy exerted a very light touch. For instance, when opened, the front door blocked the delightfully petite imperial stair. A new double-leaf door configuration now sweeps open, one leaf's hinges built to accommodate a slight variation in the floor surface without completely blocking views toward either sitting room from the entrance.

Peter and Greg salvaged a Connecticut barn to replace an original barn that had been removed prior to their ownership of Willow Hill. Positioned across the lawn and screened from the house by carefully placed trees, the repurposed barn represents an appropriate new stage in the property's evolution. Rather than graft a new addition to the main building, the couple expanded their space with an ancillary structure, much as on an early Long Island homestead.

SAGTIKOS MANOR
Islip

Sagtikos Manor is a sprawling, delightfully surreal circuit of rooms, hallways, porches, and stairs—a marriage of daffy architecture and cohesive furnishings. Last owned by Robert D. L. Gardiner, who claimed to be the sixteenth Lord of the Manor of Gardiners Island, Sagtikos is the arena where he reimagined and reinterpreted decorative and family history. His own taste and that of his family—by turns charming, unwieldy, and manic—survives and suits the house, which comprises three distinct sections dating from the seventeenth, eighteenth, and twentieth centuries.

Throughout the interior an unusually artistic array of repeating colors animate painted surfaces, patterned papers, and battered fabrics, unifying rooms that range from intimately scaled, eighteenth-century bedrooms to a twentieth-century dining room of robber baron proportions. The color of crushed pride is found throughout, complemented by a self-assured viridian that appears just as frequently as various wet sand greiges and sea lettuce greens, with oyster whites and stained woods moderating the overall palette.

But on the exterior, now stained white with dark shutters, it is evident from the varied rooflines that color alone could not unify the architectural and decorative schemes that composed, over time, a rambling farmhouse of such gargantuan scale.

The house began small and stout, built by the ambitious Stephanus Van Cortlandt, New York City's first American-born mayor. During the summer of 1697 he received not one but two manorial grants: Cortlandt along the Hudson River and Sagtikos on Long Island's southern shore. On this unusual island grant—miles long but only several hundred feet wide—he built a six-room house resembling the house later built by the Floyds of Mastic. The Hudson property received most of Van Cortlandt's attention, however, and by the Georgian era, Sagtikos was owned by the Thompsons, prosperous farmers who expanded the house. A new kitchen wing dwarfed the original kitchen, and the rest of the house was integrated into a five-bay-wide Georgian block. These rooms, all perfectly scaled for happy chats and confidential gossip, supported a façade of mildly grand pretension overlooking country fields and marshland. Its nascent sophistication greeted British troops during the Revolution, and, afterward, President Washington himself during his Long Island tour.

Walking through these comfortably scaled seventeenth- and eighteenth-century rooms today, it is a great surprise to pass through Thompson's new parlor into the soaring, cubic volume of the twentieth-century music room, as large as the entire Georgian-era addition. With its seemingly

infinite expanse of paneled wall and Arts & Crafts inglenook, this is a sudden encounter with a very different mindset. The music room was added in 1905 by Frederick Diodati Thompson, who inherited the house and commissioned architect Isaac H. Green to aggrandize the family seat in the years immediately following the Gilded Age.

Green finished the music room exterior with a deep wraparound porch, an addition that would have unbalanced the existing building if not for the massive northern wing he also designed—a gambrel-roofed appendage equivalent in volume to all the rooms already described. It connects to the older house through the original Van Cortlandt kitchen, and there is a curious moment of stepping from the early, low-ceilinged space—which Green treated as an antechamber—into the 1905 high-ceilinged stair hall, its walls covered in flamboyant peacock wallpaper. Beyond the stair hall are numerous entertaining and service rooms requested by Diodati Thompson, and upstairs are many bedrooms.

Its grand scale notwithstanding, Green's northern addition does not display the architectural hubris that Edith Wharton despised. Instead, it defers to the older parts of the house. The addition has no formal entrance, only north and south porches that speak of lingering, casual days. The addition is perpendicular to the Van Cortlandt and Thompson sections, and the music room's roofline is a continuation of those earlier sections.

Robert D. L. Gardiner inherited Sagtikos in all its delicious sprawl, complete with assorted outbuildings, garages, and a walled garden. While he also maintained a house in East Hampton, he gravitated to the grandeur of Gardiner's Island and the status of the south fork, transmuting Sagtikos into a part-time decorative and historical laboratory. A sui generis character prone to bluster, but not without charm, he appreciated the power of dramatic flair, and it is this quality that permitted him to contribute to Sagtikos's history without building another imposing wing.

Under his stewardship, the house evolved from being a family home to a museum without occupants. Yet, unlike many house museums, which are often rather humorless interpretations of a single period, this museum is a sort of wormhole, each room indelibly stamped by the time in which it was built, while connecting to past and succeeding decades through the wonderful decorative dramas of several centuries. Sagtikos's lively variety is unified by Gardiner's distinct vision, by turns serious and tongue in cheek. He brought in furniture to augment its decorative inventory and rearranged furnishings for beauty rather than historical effect—a strategy its current stewards have continued with great success. The overall effect is as salt to a meal, bringing out the house's deeper flavors of charm and history.

TURBILLON
Mill Neck

Turbillon sits on a meandering country lane overlooking gardens, pony paddocks, and shimmering Beaver Lake. It is a quintessential Long Island farmhouse with a multitude of later additions—a lovely arrangement with Colonial Revival influences. The immediate landscape contains many of the North Shore's characteristic charms, from saltwater inlets and hills shaded by deciduous trees to the gardens woven in between.

The house nestles laterally into the gentle rise of a hill, and its length reflects many stages of growth. At first glance, the lovely main block appears symmetrical but is in fact asymmetrical. Built at the start of the eighteenth century, the house was expanded several decades later when a side-hall three-bay block was added on the west. The Underhill family purchased the property in the 1760s and reconfigured the eastern wing to create a center hall.

Slowly the house grew, a metamorphosis of vernacular architecture guided by talented craftsmen and North Shore building traditions. By the end of the nineteenth century, the main block was joined to a substantial new service wing, the whole sheltered beneath a broad roof. Minimal exterior detailing gave the house a monastic simplicity, and its length belied its relatively compact nature. Inside, however, charming provincial paneling and an impressive stair hall demonstrated an exuberant attitude.

Katherine Culver Williams purchased this long, lean house in 1927. A wealthy widow from Manhattan, she embraced the farm with spirited fervor. What had formerly been a working homestead became a genteel country retreat, and Williams lavished the house with details that spoke of light and views rather than shelter and hearth. New dormer windows brought light to the third floor, and in the dining room, new French windows made a visual connection to the garden.

Best of all was the addition of a marvelous, two-story porch on the north face of the main block, the second floor screened in as a delightful sleeping porch on warm summer nights.

Resembling a rural Vermont tree house, the sleeping porch enjoys views of the blowsy grasses and trees below in grounds walled off from the road–a miniature parkland that rises up to hillside gardens. Across the lane and paddock is the lake. Formerly a tidal creek, it was flooded at the turn of the twentieth century to give local landowners a place for fishing and winter sports.

At the beginning of the twenty-first century, the nineteenth-century service wing, found to be structurally compromised, was reconfigured in a neocolonial manner, the new grafted onto the old, a further building on the efforts of previous generations. The current interiors are equally layered, the furnishings a medley of good antiques, colorful carpets, and the usual accoutrements of a life lived out of doors as much as in. The effervescent red-papered dining room, with its row of French windows showcasing the green outdoors, feels happy and assured.

For sixty years the current family has cared for this gentleperson's farm. At the top of the hill, the horse barn, chicken coop, and sheds built by Mrs. Williams have been preserved through continual use and maintenance. Though the house's namesake comes from a summer residence of the Bishops of Sion, this place of cultivated pleasure serves as a residence throughout the year, its singular atmosphere nurtured to understated excellence.

ROCK HALL
Lawrence

Rock Hall stands proud, straight, and square. It is a hierarchical composition, its assertive Georgian core flanked by a later service wing, and the whole surrounded by a garden. A fine dentiled cornice and playful Chippendale balustrade enliven, not unlike flushed cheeks and long eyelashes, what might otherwise be a handsome but severe face. Rock Hall's very name announces the home's permanence and solidity. Yet, it arose out of eighteenth-century chaos—of slave uprisings in the West Indies—and the desire to emulate the ostentation of the British landed gentry.

Like many Georgian houses in America, Rock Hall was the dream of a second son denied an inheritance under the rules of primogeniture. Josiah Martin was born in 1699 on Green Castle, the Antiguan plantation of his father, Samuel. At that time, Antigua was devoted entirely to the production of sugar cane. The life that enabled this sweet luxury was anything but, as enslaved Africans harvested the cash crop, confined by a landscape without escape routes or room to maneuver unofficial freedoms.

As brilliantly told by Shirley G. Hibbard in *Rock Hall: A Narrative History*, on Christmas Day in 1701, the Martin family's slaves revolted. Having been denied their usual holiday so that they might harvest and save that season's crop, they murdered Josiah's father. He and his siblings and mother survived, but their circumstances on that little island would be forever tenuous.

For the next thirty years Josiah worked to achieve the dream of a gentleman planter, nursing his own plantation in the hope that one day he might establish himself as an absentee planter, ensconced in a country seat in Great Britain, with a plantation manager to bear the day-to-day realities on Antigua.

A different fate intervened. While visiting his New York agent in 1731, Josiah and his young family escaped the rampant smallpox of the city with a visit to Long Island's southern shore. The allure of this rural landscape, with seemingly endless marsh and great waterway expanses leading to the Atlantic–compounded by news of another planned slave uprising in Antigua–convinced Josiah to relocate to Long Island.

In autumn 1767, as salt air came in from the bellowing Atlantic, Josiah purchased a saltwater farm that lay on the route between Hempstead and Rockaway. He quickly set about building a fashionable new house, a spare essay in smart Georgian building, a structure entirely devoted to the everyday life of his family. The family's service needs, from cooking to laundry, were accommodated in a series of haphazardly placed buildings to the east and west of the new house.

Rock Hall rose two and a half stories high with a hipped roof, its exterior ornamentation notably restrained. In contrast, the interior was lavish, with handsome paneling throughout not only the main first-floor rooms but most of the second floor as well. This was a particularly opulent touch for a man whose formative years were spent on Antigua, where such wood, like almost everything else, was an imported luxury.

Rock Hall's most dazzling interior features came about toward the end of the Martin family's ownership, with numerous elegant federal interventions. Among these, the stairs are the most impressive. The two stair halls were originally connected by a single-run stair along the middle of the first-floor hall's western wall. The insertion of a new elliptical archway in the first-floor hall now demarcated two distinct reception areas and also framed the new stairs at the southern end. With three returns and two landings, the new stairs epitomized Federal-period exuberance, with slender tapered balusters and rails terminating in minimal blunt ends. New Prussian Blue paint was applied to all wooden surfaces, promoting a luxurious sense of depth and space.

The exterior, too, was reimagined, with a new north porch and dormer windows designed with a modified ogee curve in the manner of James Gibbs. The magnificent roof balustrade, a Chinese Chippendale style, capped off the whole, its impressive lacy delight further enhancing the roof by casting delicate shadows throughout the day.

A generation after Rock Hall had evolved into the highest expression of good taste—a combined narrative of Georgian and Federal sensibilities—the property passed out of the family, purchased at auction by a young farmer, Thomas Hewlett, and his wife, Mary.

The Hewletts happily arrived, their extended family in tow, to a somewhat derelict house and immediately began stopping the onslaught of decay. The most notable external change was the relocated entrance drive, which originally wound through the property's orchards—a rather picturesque approach. The drive was replaced by a straight lane lined with trees, which still frame the house today.

Rock Hall flourished over the next several generations as the family summer house, its interior a playful mix of family heirlooms, wicker furniture, tables piled with books and candles, and windows treated with unpretentious wood blinds. Thomas's son added the eastern wing in 1881, which provided the family with up-to-date heating, electricity, and plumbing without interfering with the fabric of the original block.

The Hewletts gave Rock Hall to the stewardship of the Town of Hempstead as a museum, which attracted the passionate interest of Bertha Benkard Rose. Rose's decorative and architectural connoisseurship saved Rock Hall for the nation, albeit in a furnished manner that now seems a bit stiff for a house once used as a summer retreat. But Josiah and each subsequent generation would recognize the well-kept house today, a reminder that such places survive through effort, not luck.

Henry Lloyd Manor House, Lloyd Neck
Joseph Lloyd Manor House, Lloyd Neck

THE HENRY LLOYD AND JOSEPH LLOYD MANOR HOUSES
Lloyd Neck

Three important houses were built on the peninsular manor of Queens Village: two visible and one invisible. Enterprising Henry Lloyd built the first in 1737, a sturdy saltbox in the Connecticut saltbox tradition. Thirty years later, his proud son, Joseph, built the second, an au courant Georgian pile. Jupiter Hammon, the first published African American, enslaved by the Lloyds all his long life, built the third, not in wood but in words and stanzas. Hammon's demesne was intellectual, his inventive use of language serving as shelter for his radical, clear-sighted piety.

Henry Lloyd Manor House

Each of these houses endures today, each having been interpreted and reinterpreted by subsequent generations. It is difficult to compare these disparate legacies; indeed, it is impossible to equate them. Façades are like writings, for they are often recombinations of existing known elements—decorative details, say, or words—and then opaque, open to interpretation, their histories veiled by our knowledge or lack thereof.

Virginia Woolf observed that "words, English words, are full of echoes, of memories and associations—naturally." Jupiter Hammon worked within these echoes. Though he could not buy his freedom, he was able to buy a Bible (it is believed he was bequeathed another by his father, Obium, of Sylvester Manor) and create for himself an intellectual freedom from bondage through the vicissitudes of language. Encouraged by the Lloyds to pursue his education—it was practical to have a trusted slave with a mastery of words—he used the religiosity of his day to create poetry and writings that, though seemingly benign to his oppressors, demonstrate a clear understanding of the impossible contradiction between slavery and Christianity. He wrote in a silken language capable of eliciting white approval while slipping through white censorship, often using a royal "we" that seems to alternate between black and white-and-black:

> And now my brethren . . . to show how in some things we may be mistaken in behold-
> ing the Lamb of God while we are flattering ourselves with the hopes of salvation on
> the most slight foundation—that we live in a Christian land and attend to divine service.
> These things are good in themselves; but there must be a saving change wrought in our
> hearts" ("An Evening's Improvement").

Hammon spent the trust he accumulated from his owners to publish his work, with its hidden edicts against the crime of slavery. Almost all of his writings pursue a takedown of the sinful belief in the Elect, whispering that no group could be preordained by God to quash another's right to freedom. Yet, later generations pilloried Hammon's measured writings as those of an Uncle Tom, unaware of the defiance he wove with words in a highly restricted environment, where he and Phyllis Wheatley belonged to a tiny community publicly challenging the status quo. Only in the last few decades has his reputation been burnished by academics such as Sondra A. O'Neale, who have put his singular accomplishments into context: he straddled both the heinous period of slavery and the challenging period of manumission.

Like reputations, buildings are mutable, and the layered growth of the Lloyd manor houses reflects the desires and needs of later owners as much as the intent of the original builders.

Both the Lloyd manor houses reflect evolving aesthetic mores. The Henry Lloyd house grew in the traditional saltbox manner, extended to the north and east within the first twenty years. These additions were practical rather than grand, befitting a founder rather than an inheritor. Two hundred years later, at the beginning of the twentieth century, most of Lloyd's Neck, along with the manor house, was purchased by Marshall Field III, an inheritor of immense means. He named his estate Caumsett, and the manor house's role devolved into that of humble gatehouse for Field's holdings, then centered on a new house designed by John Russell Pope. Yet, Marshall Field did not neglect Henry Lloyd's house; he had it remodeled by the fashionable decorating firm Lenygon & Morant. The picturesque quality of the location was played up, the house treated as a delightful cottage and used by Marshall Field's second wife after their divorce.

Joseph Lloyd built his house to the west of his father's, and it showed a remarkable degree of sophistication for this relatively provincial area. A five-bay Georgian box with smart paneling wrapping formal rooms, it was a departure from the relative informality and simplicity of his father's home. By the mid-nineteenth century, Joseph's house had passed out of the Lloyd family, purchased by Mrs. Alden of New York, who used it as a summer retreat. It was likely during her tenure that large Victorian dormers were added to the south and north façades, a gracious front porch was introduced, and the service wing was expanded. Yet, her obvious façade improvements lasted only as long as her ownership.

By 1905, the house, then owned by the Wood family, was reorganized yet again. The southern Victorian dormers and front porch were removed, replaced with a neocolonial roofline with gabled dormers, the body flanked by a new west porch and garden. The current house, particularly the southern façade, is simple yet imbued with too many evolutionary jumps for a purely colonial house. Now owned by Preservation Long Island, its current incarnation—a combination of colonial, Georgian, Victorian, and contemporary eras—is a stealthy reinvention of the past, which some people, in passing, might mistakenly regard as a wholly traditional colonial house.

Henry Lloyd Manor House

Henry Lloyd Manor House

Henry Lloyd Manor House

Joseph Lloyd Manor House

Joseph Lloyd Manor House

Joseph Lloyd Manor House

THATCH MEADOW FARM
Head of the Harbor

As a small child, Constance "Conky" Nostrand would climb to the third floor of her grandmother's house to peer through one of the little dormer windows that festooned the roof. Absorbed by the view of placid bay water, she would steer an antique spinning wheel, set just below the window, and ply a pirate ship through tumultuous seas in search of treasure. Her shingle-clad ship, the house at the center of Thatch Meadow Farm, was the long-held prize of her shrewd, self-reliant grandmother, Viola Courtenay Billings.

Billings's triumphant ownership of Thatch Meadow Farm capped years of careful investing and arduous work: over several decades she grew a small bank into a regional powerhouse. Majestically sited, the property encompasses a series of orchards, meadows, and undulating lawns, as well as a grand barn quadrangle, cottages, and an eighteenth-century farmhouse with nineteenth- and twentieth-century additions. The whole overlooks a great expanse of thatch meadows and the harbor. Billings celebrated her purchase of the property by buying a diamond ring, picked up during a trip to South Africa.

The main house, originally built by the Smith family in the eighteenth century, was later extended in the Federal style. It is an example of an unusual type of house once found along the North Shore. It is constructed directly in front of a hill for protection from northern winds, with a glacial stone retaining wall carving out space between the building and the hill. A bridge spans the two, connecting the upper floors with the hillside. Thus it is possible to walk from the golden saltwater meadows in front of the house, across the lawn, and into the main hall. Then, clasping the elegantly lean Federal stair rail, you ascend to a second-floor hall similar to the one below and proceed to exit straight through an attractive, early-nineteenth-century doorway into an enclosed, porch-like bridge, which releases you to the hillside and its fish pond and fire pits beyond. When you look back, the house appears as an outgrowth of the hill itself.

Billings purchased Thatch Meadow in good repair, maintained to a glorious standard by its former owner, George Bacon. In 1912 he commissioned Peabody, Wilson & Brown to renovate the existing structures and build new cottages and a clock tower. Bacon's architectural commission added a bit of refinement to an already charming house, with stylized Ionic columns added throughout. Best of all was a new enclosed sunroom that transforms into a veranda via oversized windows that descend into the lower half of the wall.

From the bedroom terrace above the sunroom, it is possible to survey the breadth of the property. To the west is the bay, with its whirling grasses. To the east is the roof of the northern wing, containing the original cookhouse; its roofline appears to merge with several cottages and the distant barns. The illusion resembles a bucolic hamlet, strung between folds of field surrounded by wood.

Billings, a keen horticulturalist, composed a series of axial gardens that served as an orderly foreground to pasture populated by sheep, ground formerly populated by Bacon's Guernsey cattle. She had an eye for understated beauty and filled the rooms of her house with spare wood and wicker antiques. These were later joined by Nostrand's older sister's paintings and countless ceramics made by her late husband, Guy Hilbert. The latter are displayed to great effect in a second-floor sunroom that floods with afternoon light.

Like her grandmother, Nostrand harbors a profound love for Thatch Meadow Farm. She has been indefatigable in managing the estate, ensuring the buildings' longevity and maintaining the grounds' understated atmosphere. The entrance dirt road remains perfectly as is—a mix of pebbles and earth that seamlessly blends into the landscape—and the property boundaries remain delineated by neighborly natural hedges and undergrowth.

It often happens that treasure turns up beneath our feet. So it has been for Nostrand, who wears her grandmother's diamond ring—a symbol of union to Thatch Meadow—as only a natural chatelaine can.

HAY FEVER
Locust Valley

Some houses are praised as timeless, connoting an airy, unplaceable, and presumably universal sense of taste. Others are more self-assured, commanding our passionate attention through their loyalty to details of place and history. Hay Fever is such a house. Perched on a gentle knoll just outside the Gold Coast hamlet of Locust Valley, this penultimate Long Island farmhouse has sheltered generations of remarkable aesthetes.

The usual approach to Hay Fever is oblique, passing a copse of elm, locust, and beech tamed into controlled yet poetic disarray, accompanied by the crunch of pea gravel underfoot. The house's variegated profile is slowly revealed as the rambler it is: the main block rises over two subsidiary wings that stretch northward to form a garden court. Each twist and turn in plan—a historic building sequence spanning several centuries—humanizes the house and draws you in, beckoning you to walk past the neat allées and enter through the north Dutch door—the upper half always flung open in good weather—crowned by antlers mounted á la Hubert de Givenchy's Château du Jonchet. The former residence of Jane Robinson Teller, "the Unsung Queen of the Colonial Revival" (*New York Times*), and later Edith Hay Wyckoff, "the Gadfly of the Gold Coast" (*Newsday*), Hay Fever is now home to designer Jeffrey Bilhuber. Stepping inside, one instantly beholds a uniquely alluring place of twentieth- and twenty-first-century creative reinvention.

Yet, Hay Fever's story begins a century before the Revolutionary War, when Long Island was wholly rural, a bountiful terrain of fertile land surrounded by creeks, coves, and bays teeming with maritime life. Here, on a knoll in a shallow valley on the island's North Shore, the Underhill family built a very simple house in 1668. As family fortunes improved and the wealth of new owners intervened, the original house grew. Eventually it became outmoded and was adapted to new use as a subservient kitchen wing for a side-hall house built by the Cocks, an old Quaker family who bought the Underhills' modest homestead around 1790.

As each harvest yielded to another and one colony joined many to form a new nation, the house prospered with new purpose. Education came to the valley during the 1840s, when Lot Cornelius purchased the property as a home for his Walnut Grove Seminary. He too expanded the house to accommodate his future students. It took on a more sophisticated air, with bays added to the main block, creating a handsome central-hall configuration. Its new confidence was capped by a third story delineated by a smart band of frieze windows, a subtle allusion to urbane notions of the architectural orders. The whole structure remained wrapped in the traditional, lengthy shingles of Long Island that had sheathed the original small building.

Eighty years on, the rumble of the twentieth century arrived at Hay Fever in the guise of Mr. and Mrs. Teller from New York, Colonial Revivalists hunting for a country house retreat. They added an eastern wing to balance the kitchen wing, thereby increasing the length of the southern façade and creating a U-shaped courtyard, improvements possibly suggested by the prolific architect Maurice Fatio.

From the house the Tellers ran the Stage Coach Inn, an immersive reimagining of colonial Americana. As Wallace Nutting and Martha Stewart would do decades later, they forged an aesthetic as approachable as it was intoxicating, in their case a heady nostalgia for America's colonial past. Guests would be greeted by Mrs. Robinson in period costume and then were free to wander through the Mount Vernon Room and dine in the Independence Hall Room before leaving with a souvenir piece of pewter (stamped with an anagram of Mrs. Teller's name). Henry Fonda, James Stewart, and Christopher Morley, who performed at the nearby Red Barn Theatre, all were visitors.

The inn closed before the start of WWII, abandoned and bereft until the Hays purchased it and rechristened it Hay Fever, after the Noel Coward play. From one of its rooms their tenacious daughter, Edith, launched her newspaper the *Locust Valley Leader*, which assumed regional importance because of her determination. If the Tellers represented the past, reprising history through deft interior decoration, Edith represented the present, commenting on society to create something of importance for the coming years. Hay Fever was a place of passion where she crusaded for the founding of the local Boys and Girls club, organized citizens against Robert Moses's proposed Long Island Sound Bridge, and always found time to question the local school board.

After Edith's death, her caretakers, the McCoys, inherited the house and sold it to local antiques dealer Roland Cotter-Kroboth. He had rightly assumed that developers would circle the once-again-frayed old house, and labored to save it until a new owner could be found to oversee its rebirth.

Jeffrey Bilhuber, a designer known for his consummately achieved interiors, stepped in to revive the faded majesty of Hay Fever, the perfect canvas for his particular creative brilliance. With the gentlest touch, Bilhuber conserved original windows and floors and sacrificed nothing that was delightful. His thoughtful interventions—redirecting the drive along the southern front with landscape designer Nancy Goslee Power, creating a proper entrance hall with powder room, and reconfiguring the eastern wing as a master bedroom befitting such a house—harmonize so beautifully with the existing fabric as to feel inevitable rather than forced.

Yet, nothing is inevitable with an old house, and it is a wonderful testament to Bilhuber's taste that he has filled Hay Fever with a delightful assortment of furniture, wallpapers, and objects unlikely to have been bettered by anything in the past. This, truly, is Hay Fever's magic: imbued with layers of history, it moves forward still. Its present is the best stage yet.

CEDARMERE
Roslyn

William Cullen Bryant revelled in the glorious possibilities of an artfully composed life. Variously described as a poet, writer, lawyer, traveler, progressive champion, and horticulturist, he was first and foremost a Romantic. Among Romantics, however, Bryant was in many ways the odd man out. Other Romantics sought in nature an escape from a vexing present day: Henry David Thoreau retreated physically by playing hermit in the woods, while James Fenimore Cooper escaped intellectually, writing tales of an imagined American past set in the country's majestic landscapes. Bryant, in contrast, saw nature not as a means of escape but rather as a reality to savor. For him, pleasure and righteousness were not in conflict but, rather, two halves of a whole.

As editor of the *New York Evening Post*, where he advocated for unions and the abolitionist movement, Bryant had long wished for a country house where he could observe, explore, and interpret the natural world. Though tempted by the beauty of the Hudson River valley—he was an early proponent of that school of painting and a friend of Thomas Cole—he chose instead the variegated landscape of Long Island's North Shore.

Artistic representation records what is believed as much as what is seen. Painters of the Hudson River school, such as Frederic Edwin Church, observed immense views, creating a canon of art that portrayed a vast, sublime wilderness stretching across the horizon. Their brushstrokes rendered people as minor, errant interlopers in nature. In contrast, during this same period artists of the North Shore, such as William Sidney Mount, worked outside a cohesive, fashionable school, observing the North Shore's alluring variety of scales. These alternate between the reassuring middle scale of views across a few miles of Long Island Sound to the Connecticut shoreline—not Earth's horizon many miles distant—and the still-smaller scale of saltwater coves and wooded hollows in temperate valleys. Found within the latter is the most intimate landscape of all: the buildings where people live their lives. People figure prominently in the foreground. The North Shore suited Bryant's outlook and served as a landscape frame for his primary interests: people and plants.

In 1834 he purchased Cedarmere, a 1700s Quaker homestead, from a friend. The main house included in the sale was, for Bryant, almost an afterthought, a ready-made folly for taking in the panoptic view. From the house it was possible to see fields, orchards, copse, woods, marsh, and beach.

Bryant redesigned the property with a connoisseur's palate and an artist's eye, a poem written not in words but cultivated in land. Whereas Thoreau's wilderness reflected a schism between progress and man, Bryant's cultivated landscape demonstrated their union. He was fond of trees and propagated a salon of the best: locust, tulip, persimmon, chicksaw plum, mulberry, pear, cherry, and many others, some from Oyster Bay and others from as far afield as Greece.

To the main house Bryant brought lightness and simplicity, removing a cornice and pillars and replacing them with latticework to encourage the growth of vines on the façade. During Bryant's son's ownership, a fire decimated much of the house above the first floor. His son rebuilt the facade with erratic window bay projections, mercifully brought to heel by the re-created latticework.

The aesthetic of Andrew Jackson Downing's Gothic Revival, and the belief in beauty for all, found expression in the numerous buildings that Bryant added to the property for entertaining a creative coterie of well-known friends including Cooper, Cole, and actor Edwin Booth. He also invited his favorite local neighbors to live in the picturesque cottages he built amid the seemingly endless gardens.

Yet, in all of this landscape it is the Mill, which floats between millpond and harbor, that epitomizes Bryant's Romantic attitude. Clad in Gothic attractions and serving as the property's focal point, the Mill is emblematic of his belief that productivity need not defeat elegance and nature.

CARHART HOUSE
Lattingtown

The North Shore's winding lanes weave between many wooded thickets. Occasional breaks in the growth provide glimpses of campestral vistas, where wide lawn and sinewy field wash over the terrain. The scene appears unchanging, imbued with a consistent calm. Yet, in the shadow of this tranquility is a landscape that, like many others, has reflected the whims of various individuals over time.

The most mythic example is the lost hamlet of Lattingtown, partially razed in 1900 by William Guthrie to make way for his sprawling estate, Meudon. C. P. H. Gilbert designed a ponderous house at its center, one that reflected an exceedingly academic take on the Beaux-Arts style. It was a building without aesthetic or material connection to its environment. The interiors were a world of unrelieved excess, Empire furniture without imperial splendor. The grounds, vast terraces lined by arch, formal gardens, were meant to impress rather than envelope family and visitors. Unsurprisingly, like its French namesake, Meudon no longer exists; it lasted for fewer than six decades before being swept away.

Still other buildings rose in Meudon's midst, early-twentieth-century houses poised for longevity. The great tide of the Colonial Revival movement left a sea of flotsam in its wake; the best new houses of this ilk were based on a close reading of vernacular precedent. Carhart House, constructed two decades after Meudon, is an unusually thoughtful arrangement. It is massed asymmetrically, a reference to the gradual process of growth consonant with the evolution of many houses of colonial origin. Its grander exterior elements—notably a portico of imposing height—are, like pearl studs worn immediately after a swim, a no-nonsense flamboyance that requires deftness to pull off.

Amusingly, the interiors possess many of Guthrie's hoped-for attributes. Here is a masterful union of the designer Frank de Biasi with the erudite owners, who sought to create a breezy, low-key refinement. A sophisticated assortment of European elements lends the rooms good posture. Furnishings such as Adnet chairs and an antique bombe secretary are treated casually rather than sycophantically. Brilliant Portuguese needlepoint carpets ground many of the rooms with well-mannered ease. The furnishings are integrated without fuss, effectively anchoring these rooms within the wider pantheon of twentieth-century North Shore interiors, exhibiting the gravity of Thelma Chrysler Foy's Locust Valley retreat at one end and the cleverness of Horst P. Horst's Oyster Bay house at the other. The overall effect feels wonderfully adroit, enhancing comfort with the trappings of erudition, and is completed by views through blue-shuttered windows toward the rolling grounds.

"We're always buying trees," remarked one of the current owners, and it shows in the arboreal quality of the grounds, designed in consultation with Nany Taylor. Trees flank the north drive leading to the house, proudly sited at the top of a knoll overlooking the cascading grounds below. To the south, rising above the house, are a series of gardens united by vistas framed by many more trees as well as hedges and vines. The house's two-story portico, with an enclosed piazza, reinforces a tight union between outdoors and indoors. Its polished confines provoke you to meditate on the spectacular views, down a plush lawn toward the distant, shimmering pond.

OLD MASTIC
Mastic

Old Mastic, seen from a distance, is a wave of white clapboard cresting over a broad field. Unified and stolid, its long southern façade overlooks land that stretches uninterrupted toward the bay. A feeling of unhurried permanence pervades the scene. Yet, behind the cohesive front is an elegant puzzle of a house, a history of additions and accretions hinted at by two curious northern extensions: a long, sinewy wing with summer kitchen and porches above, and a low, muscular wing that stays low to the ground. The particular nostalgia evinced by the house today is not the delicacy of Proust's madeleine dipped in tea, but a hardier aura of slightly burnt toast followed by a run through the fields. Elegance in thought is tempered by affability in expression.

The southern façade is that of a saltbox with ambition: seven major bays along the central block, flanked by an early extension, present an imposing length to visitors. In plan, the house is an upside-down π, and what the writer Donald Eberlein dismissed as "several unimportant verandahs tacked on in the nineteenth century" are among its most-charming features; they are also important to understanding the house's architectural evolution and transformation of purpose. Inherited by a signer of the Declaration of Independence, this is an example of an American country house, formerly a center of provincial political power and influence, that evolved into a hunting retreat for subsequent generations.

William Floyd inherited the estate from his father, whose own father purchased it during the seventeenth century from the romantically named "Tangier" Smiths of St. George's Manor. Located on Mastic Neck, a grand sweep of forest and burgeoning fields surrounded by lavish marshes, and, farther on, the waters of Shinnecock Bay, its hedges and ditches still delineate field and woods known to Floyd 200 years ago. The grounds immediately surrounding the house have changed more extensively, principally through the movement of ancillary buildings to their current location north of the main house.

Today we can see confident, specific accretions that acknowledge the original house but neither kowtow to it nor overwhelm it. Until 1790, the house had consisted of five proper bays: the original, not insubstantial eastern section of two floors and attic, as well as a later addition often described as an unusually wide center hall. It is, in fact, a proper hall in the English tradition, a gathering place almost as wide as it is deep. To this whole, two more bays were added, creating a grander total of seven, along with new eastern and western wings depicted in a portrait of Floyd painted by Ralph Earl in 1791–92.

Later generations continued to build. The western wing as seen in the Earle portrait was removed; various dormers were sprinkled on the roofs; and a front porch with simple, robust square columns was added, a fashionable place for family and guests to gather in summer. During the nineteenth century, northern wings were unfurled: the family reconfigured the existing kitchen wing and, later, at the close of that century, added a second northern wing complete with summer sleeping porch. Both wings overlook the group of accumulated farm structures to the north. Everything was reworked with one eye on practicality, the other on loveliness. Perhaps the most endearing embellishment is the interior louvered doors, seldom seen in the region, which line the common room above the downstairs hall, permitting cooling winds to blow throughout the bedrooms.

The interior seen today remains as it was during its genteel zenith, used by the family as a country retreat until 1975. Strong colors and delicate prints are overlaid on generations of heirlooms. Heavy Empire furniture is relieved by rather more fanciful older and younger pieces: sconces topped with schooner-lined paper shades and oil portraits line the walls. In the library, piles of books still await readers beneath an eccentric cabal of taxidermied animals. These contents imbue the rooms with the clarity of a daydream, permitting visitors to conjure memories of long summer days, echoes of banging screen doors, and the astringent scent of the distant sea.

CASA BLANCA
Lattingtown

At Casa Blanca the confident reign of high summer never seems in doubt. For months on end, iridescent light from an ebullient sun and a humidity like velvet on the skin persist. People revel outdoors with sun-kissed temples and dewy nape of neck. The occasional rain shower, precipitated by a quick breeze, breaks up the otherwise halcyon months of warmth.

But eventually a clear night always arrives, and with it a chilly breeze augurs rumor of change. Days and weeks unfold with nothing coming to pass. Then, suddenly, it happens. Autumn overtakes summer, its arrival heralded by a mighty display of citrine, amber, and crimson foliage, hypnotic colors that wash away the memory of summer's steady green.

It was during this prismatic season at the end of the eighteenth century that Casa Blanca's builder was born. Peter Cock came into the world at the hamlet Killingworth upon Matinecock on the homestead established during the 1660s by his merchant-adventurer great-great-grandfather James. Throughout the Killingworth neighborhood, from the time of James onward, a series of Long Island farmhouses were built in the accretive, regional form distinctive to the area.

Though Peter grew up surrounded by houses constructed in this fashion, he fell under the influence of the nationally prominent Federal style. A successful farmer by middle age, he sought to showcase his prosperity and family's standing by erecting a new, assertive house of three stories. Built in the Federal style and five bays wide, with a smaller service wing to the west, it was clad in long shingles whose minute shadows mitigated the severity of its façade. A band of third-floor frieze windows, emphasized by a provincial architrave of thin wooden bands, projected calm and order. A southern porch with Tuscan columns spanned the middle length of the main block and served as a place for family and visitors to gather, overlooking the fields and a dirt road beyond. Like his Quaker grandfather, Peter was noted for his hospitality. His new house offered a multitude of reception rooms as well as many bedrooms on the second and third floors.

Peter's and his son George Washington's generations were the last of the family to enjoy the original homestead. Yet, the spirit of George Washington's namesake would return in the guise of Colonial Revival gentrification only a generation later. At the beginning of the twentieth century, the homestead was sold to new owners, who proceeded to give the house and grounds a Colonial Revival makeover complete with all the trimmings of a gentleperson's farm.

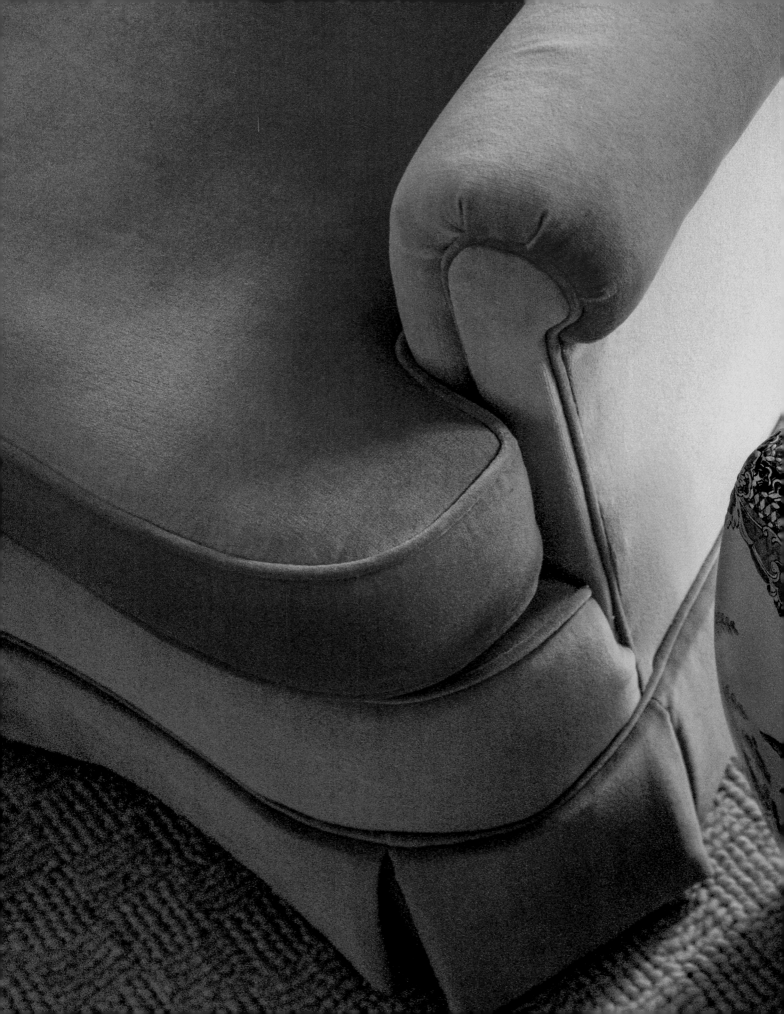

Beyond the old orchard, the new owners added an attractive group of service buildings in the vein of the increasingly de rigueur farm group, including barns with stalls for eleven horses, dog kennels, small shops, and a pump house. A superintendent's house and companion cottage rounded out the compound. Immediately next to the house, a large walled garden was added to the north, along with a handsome vegetable garden and ancillary sheds shielded by evergreens. The grounds around the house were refined: rolling lawns were introduced and ivy was encouraged to climb the new brick walls that separated the various gardens.

The new owners renovated with an eye to early-twentieth-century visions of hospitality. A new portico in the manner of Mount Vernon was erected across the front; the third-floor frieze windows were elongated into casement windows to permit more light to enter the bedrooms. The small service wing, which likely subsumed whatever earlier homestead structure was on the site, was enlarged, with servants' bedrooms added above reconfigured service rooms.

Today, Casa Blanca's interiors exude steadfast calm; no element is superfluous. A tranquil palette of waxed woods and creamy paint dominate most rooms. The capacious floors are unified by a marvelous stair that winds from the first floor to the third, the handrail looping at each landing in a return swoop, floating on slender, painted bannisters.

The third-floor bedrooms offer the best views of the seasonal drama outside. Their cozy window seats, with cushions upholstered in bittersweet stripe, overlook the gentle leaves gathering on the lawn, shaped like a shallow bowl. At the center of the action is an explosive evergreen, its branches flaring toward the changing sky.

POINT PLACE
Miller Place

People gather instinctively around old houses, which, more than any book, remind us very concretely that we are a part of history; that history is never as remote as it seems but is suffused with memories of laughter, whispers, and inquiry, with long stares and parting glances connecting us all in time. Point Place, securely situated on a bluff at the end of a hollow overlooking Mount Sinai Harbor, has long been a point of unity for its families and community.

Today, light still streams through six-over-six sash windows, washing over family and friends as they chat in rooms appointed with beautiful antique furniture and lively, pungently painted trim: moss green, charred tomato red. The overall effect is calm but not sedate. The whole sits under a proper cedar shake roof, a testament to the enduring charm of material choices informed by tradition and aesthetics alike.

For 200 years, from 1754 to the mid-twentieth century, Point Place belonged to the Hopkins family. Theirs was a world of long summers and long winters spent on more than a thousand farming acres running north toward the sound. Samuel Hopkins, born on Shelter Island and descended from a Mayflower émigré, purchased a little over a hundred acres two decades before the Revolution. He was the first of his family to modify and adjust the house already sited on the bluff, surrounded by an expanse of waterside farmland amenable to the shipment of goods, with a view no less impressive then than now.

The house we see today, like others nearby, originated with its older, minor wing (ca. 1720). This portion is one-half of the original house, which Hopkins split in two, keeping half on the existing site and moving the other half elsewhere on his newly purchased homestead. As the Hopkins family grew, the remaining portion was expanded and eventually grafted, in 1770, onto a new, fashionable, five-bay-wide Georgian block. This new addition, two rooms wide, two rooms deep, and two and a half stories high, with a bit of lateral sprawl echoing that of the earlier wing, indicates success in farming and shipping as much as an awareness of Anglo-American architectural fashion. Though Great Britain was politically on its way out in the colonies, increasingly flummoxed by upstart colonists, its cultural and aesthetic grip would remain.

In 1816, the now American Hopkins family chose to update their predominantly Georgian-era house and, like many families on the island, did so in the airier Federal style, an American variant of the neoclassical style championed by the Scottish brothers and architects Robert and James Adam. While purely Federal houses are often vaguely pedantic—albeit beautiful—essays in pattern book geometry, houses updated in the Federal style often emphasize its best attributes, which include a dominance of plain surfaces complemented by shallow relief details and an overall quest for lightness. The reinvented Federal style escaped the domineering effect of severe exterior compositions and excessive, often-anemic interior ornament. Late Federal is an ideal finishing-school style, and the Hopkins family updated their house to underscore its most-elegant aspects.

The main southern door was embellished with a new elliptical fanlight with sidelights, permitting sunlight to flood the main hall. Ceiling moldings added to the reception rooms bring impressive visual interest, and all the main windows were replaced by six-over-six sash windows with slender muntins, allowing the family to bask in every drop of daylight.

The homestead truly became its own world, and as the house expanded, a mix of outbuildings proliferated over the burgeoning farm. A smokehouse, icehouse, boathouse, and numerous barns indicated a commercial connection with distant New York yet remained emblematic of the family's roots in the thinly populated tidal countryside.

In 1940, Point Place was purchased by a New York City family, who enjoyed it as a summer house for a quarter of a century. It was then sold twice in the span of a decade before being purchased by the current owner, the antiquarian and aesthete Robert Arnold. The house has benefited from his family's full-time occupation and restoration, and its current state reflects both reverence for the past and reimagination for the present.

The outlook from the house remains magnificent. The southern view across tidal marsh toward the woods was preserved through the community's effort to balance rather than thwart the hamlet's post-WWII growth.

A medley of ancillary buildings near the house still stands, lording it over the paddocks and lawns. The magnificent barn has long been home to ponies that enjoy a saltwater marsh jaunt along with generations of children. More recently the second floor of an old boathouse was repurposed as a pool house, very much in the spirit of the traditional repurposing and moving of old wood-frame buildings. Their presence complements the house, which remains a treasured survivor of many epochs, a steadfast repository of memories and future aspirations alike.

SYLVESTER MANOR
Shelter Island

Two entrance piers—solid, serious, and chalk white—mark
the current route to Sylvester Manor. These twentieth-
century additions stand sentry over the beginning of a drive
that plunges into forest, then meanders through the growth.
Sound is softened by textures in the tree canopies overhead
and on the forest floor underfoot. The warm, sharp smells of
decomposing matter fill the nostrils. This sequence, which
appears to let nature have her way, is a palate cleanse for the
visitor, one no less contrived than an allée.

Slowly the forest recedes, animal pastures come into view,
and barns begin to appear. The drive then swings out from the
forest and begins a final march toward the manor house, cutting
a swath through lawns and passing centuries of old boxwood
before culminating at the southern front of the manor.

The house is wonderfully inviting: two large chimney stacks balance a flared hip roof atop a symmetrical façade with shuttered sash windows. Pilasters frame the block, flanked in turn by side verandas. It is an appealing, genteel, and unmistakably domestic façade. It overlooks the drive, which extends back toward the forest that long ago reclaimed evidence of the once-sprawling commercial plantation–an enterprise that underpinned the manor and supported its rise.

Today the property is a singular example of its type, a manorial domain on which a northern plantation house was built that, like many southern plantation houses after the Civil War, now wears a Colonial Revival cloak. Its current appearance, by turns proud and self-effacing, dates from its transition into a country house for leisure at the beginning of the twentieth century.

Successive waves of architectural fashion are visible across and throughout the house, all superimposed by successive generations of the Sylvester descendents. The dominant features– namely, the elegant roofline and handsome chimneys–remain as they were when Brinley Sylvester wished them into being. In 1737, he gained ownership of a thousand-acre holding on Shelter Island after a protracted legal case against his uncle. Brinley knocked down the old manor house that accompanied the land, built by his grandfather during the third quarter of the seventeenth century, and erected a new house in the Georgian style. It was likely inspired by George Berkeley's Whitehall outside Newport, itself inspired by Palladio's ideas as filtered through the mid-eighteenth-century generation of English gentleman-builders. Later generations would bring a more casual élan to the house, importing their own ideas about how it should be organized. Always respectful of the southern façade's symmetry, they expanded the house northward in a practical jumble of rooms, reconfigured by the architect Henry Bacon at the beginning of the twentieth century.

Bacon, employed by Cornelia Horsford, inheritor of Sylvester Manor at that time, did much more than simply rearrange a few rear rooms. Before embarking on a Colonial Revival invigoration, Bacon made a comprehensive record of the structure as it was; he was an architect finely attuned to how architectural traces of the past exhibit a special romance. Horsford and Bacon's reinterpretation achieved the house we see today: a main block bookended by verandas, a front door with a small portico replacing the 1840s front porch, and the reorganization of the north rooms around a new living room. The senior Horsfords, pillars of Cambridge society, were scientists of reason, in contrast to their romantically inclined daughter, Cornelia. They inscribed a boulder near the burying ground as memorial to the buried slaves and natives from the active plantation years. Cornelia sought to enshrine the nobility of an earlier era, advocating for a marker denoting the place where Chief Sachem Youghco's funeral procession purportedly rested during its progression to Montauk in 1652.

Sitting in the parlor chamber filled with solid furniture enhanced by the patina of time, all set off by late-nineteenth-century Zuber wallpaper, your gaze inevitably follows sunlight to the floor and out into the hall, toward the precocious Victorian stair, its slow rise indicating an unhurried step. When your gaze returns to the parlor, it might light on the room's northeast corner, behind which lies the steep, unlit service stair used by servants and slaves alike. Each room in the house offers similar glimpses of beauty entangled with thorns of the past.

Majestic Gardiners Creek still shimmers to the west of the house, and to the north, south, and east the land surrounding the manor has been preserved by the Sylvester family as a nonprofit focused on education and culture. The land is now farmed under the community-supported agriculture model. There has been no overzealous restoration of the grounds immediately surrounding the house, which, though witness to archeological digs and a new family agenda, still possess an unruffled, timeworn quality that suits the spirit of the place. Gently stewarded into the twenty-first century for more than fifty years by Andrew and Alice Fiske, it was then gifted by Eben Fiske Ostby and his family to the community in 2014. The house remains well loved, a lasting testament to the gravity of history and ambition.

TERRY-MULFORD HOUSE
Orient

The North Fork is a long, agrarian stretch of land between Long Island Sound and the Peconic and Gardiner Bays. It narrows eastward, reaching one final expansion, a triumphant flex of field and marsh that rapidly contracts and ends at Orient Point. Gliding along the main road, before approaching the water's edge, the Terry-Mulford House comes into view. It is one of Orient's oldest houses—indeed, perhaps one of the oldest privately inhabited houses in New York State.

A grand saltbox, the Terry-Mulford's main block is Puritan New England in character, tempered by a front porch ease, courtesy of a nineteenth-century addition. The composition is completed by the startling pomp of a wing constructed in naive twentieth-century Tudor Revival style. Elinor Latham Williams, the elegant and unpretentious mistress of the house for the past forty years, referred to these portions, respectively, as Old House, Middle House, and Big House. The simplicity of this description and its satisfying rhythm has the plain charm of a nursery rhyme yet hints at a more complex story.

Old House looks out across the road and waving grasses, surrounded by bucolic farmland. Most passersby, breezily on their way to village or ferry, are drawn to the home's esteemed demeanor but remain unaware of its rarity: it is the only plank-walled house in New York. The entire structure—timbers, planks, internal walls, siding—is built entirely of white oak. The extravagance of this material choice suggests that the surrounding landscape was at one time very different.

Forest once covered today's farmland. White oak, prized during the seventeenth century as a material for stave blanks, formed part of the earliest colonial Atlantic trade route. Vintners valued the material's ability to breathe, useful in aging wine, and so it was exported from Orient to the Azores, Madeira, and the Canary Islands in exchange for wine, which was then traded in London for manufactured items, which in turn came back to the island. Old House benefited from the wide availability of this material and possibly served as a barracks for its harvest, if not built for that express purpose.

But the forests of Long Island were quickly plundered, and by the third quarter of the seventeenth century, many towns prohibited tree cutting for trade. Eventually, as settlements formed, the region assumed an agricultural air, and during the early 1700s, Williams's seventh-great-grandfather purchased the property. He expanded the house, adding a lean-to, a practical buttery, and a much-grander two-unit front door to accommodate a reconfigured stair.

The house eventually passed to the Mulfords, who built Middle House around 1820, truly a distinctly second house grafted onto the first, to accommodate a multigenerational family. Middle House now constitutes the introduction to the entire configuration, with visitors passing across its front porch into the calm of the inner sitting room. A curious door with a diamond-paned window, located on a party wall shared with Old House, provides an astonishing through-the-looking-glass moment: when opened, it reveals a magnificent, relatively intact seventeenth-century interior. Where Middle House serves as a sort of calm, sedate, everyday dwelling, Old House is a more complex aesthete's delight, a private museum filled with locally made furniture from the eighteenth and nineteenth centuries.

Williams, raised at Latham Farm in Orient, and long familiar with the house originally purchased by her seventh-generation great-grandfather, recalled visiting its then owners during her childhood on the rural North Fork. A descendent both of the Mulford and Terry families, she left Orient as a young woman for a spell in China before Mao came to power, then spent several years on the West Coast and in Pennsylvania.

Yet, Orient never lost its appeal, and when she learned that her ancestral property was up for sale in 1979, she purchased it with her second husband, Ralph O. Williams. Together they restored the neglected house to its splendid present-day state. They filled the garden with flowers, blueberries, and asparagus and furnished the fantastical interiors with their eclectic collections.

They renewed Old House first, furnishing its marvelously preserved entertaining rooms with furniture either made on Long Island or long held by the island's families. Middle House accommodated Williams's culinary expertise, and, not for the first time in its history, the kitchen was reconfigured, this time for meals of scrumptious Chinese food and delicious pies and cobblers made from the fruits of Orient's agricultural bounty. Big House saw the insertion of a new library, and the largest room—formerly a painting gallery—accommodated Ralph's copious collection of antique radios. Slowly the house emerged anew through their inspired stewardship.

To swan about the house today, to pass through each century of the last 400 years, is to feel like Lewis Carroll's Alice lingering in the golden gleam, never doubting the Williams's dream.

ACKNOWLEDGMENTS

With heartfelt thanks to the many owners and stewards of the houses and properties depicted in this book: Robert Arnold, Peter Bickford and Greg McCarthy, Jeffrey Bilhuber, Harriet Gerard Clark, Kevin and Alice Concagh, the Deans family, the Friends of Cedarmere, William P. J. Gooth, Jennifer Smith Huntley, MaryLaura Lamont, the Lloyd Harbor Historical Society, Eben Fiske Ostby and family, Richard C. Martin, William Miller and Mary Abbene, Joan McGee, Thomas U. Powell, Constance "Conky" Nostrand, Lisa W. Ott, Preservation Long Island, William Floyd Estate, Fire Island National Seashore, the North Shore Land Alliance, National Park Service, Town of Hempstead, Raynham Hall Museum, Suffolk County Parks Division of Historic Services, Sylvester Manor Educational Farm, Elinor Latham Williams, Alexandra Wolfe, Youngs Farm, and those who wish to remain fashionably anonymous.

Enormous thanks to my editor, Cheryl Weber, for advocating on behalf of this project, and to Peter Schiffer, Danielle D. Farmer, and the entire Schiffer Publishing team for bringing this book to fruition.

Particular thanks to William Miller for graciously writing the foreword, Lisa Zeiger for kindly reading my first draft and offering astute suggestions, and Jacqueline Anerella for brilliantly designing a mockup of the book.

Unending thanks to my marvelous parents, Mark and Debra, my lovely family and good-humored friends, and my partner, Matt Smoak, for offering a critical eye and kind words in equal measure.

And my gratitude to Zehra Ahmed, Stephen Bastone, Calvin Churchman, John Collins, Suzanne Dannan, East Hampton Historical Society, Library of Congress, James Huvane, Barbara Van Liew, Locust Valley Historical Society, Locust Valley Library, Metropolitan Museum of Art, Miller Place Historical Society, New York Public Library, Oyster Bay Historical Society, Oyster Bay Library, Oyster Ponds Historical Society, Kate Pfeiffer, Preservation Long Island, Tom Samet, Smithtown Library, SUNY Stony Brook Library, Sanjay Kumar Verma, Bunny Williams, and those who cherish our world.

RESOURCES

East Hampton Historical Society
www.easthamptonhistory.org

Friends of Cedarmere
www.friendsofcedarmere.org/index.html

Friends of Rock Hall
www.friendsofrockhall.org

Lloyd Harbor Historical Society
www.lloydharborhistoricalsociety.org

Locust Valley Historical Society
www.locustvalleyhistory.org

Long Island Museum
www.longislandmuseum.org

National Park Service
www.nps.gov/index.htm

North Shore Land Alliance
www.northshorelandalliance.org

Oyster Bay Historical Society
www.oysterbayhistorical.org

Oyster Ponds Historical Society
www.oysterpondshistoricalsociety.org

Peconic Land Trust
www.peconiclandtrust.org

Preservation Long Island
www.preservationlongisland.org

Raynham Hall
www.raynhamhallmuseum.org

Rock Hall
www.friendsofrockhall.org

Sagtikos Manor
www.sagtikosmanor.org

Smithtown Library
www.smithlib.org

SUNY Stony Brook
www.stonybook.edu

Sylvester Manor Educational Farm
www.sylvestermanor.org

William Floyd Estate
www.nps.gov

Youngs Farm
https://youngs.farm

BIBLIOGRAPHY

Baker, Anthony, Robert B. MacKay, and Carol A. Traynor, eds. *Long Island Country Houses and Their Architects, 1860–1940.* New York: W. W. Norton, 1997. pp. 332–44.

Bedford, Steven M. "Country and City: Some Formal Comparisons." In *The Long Island Country House, 1870–1930.* Edited by Parrish Art Museum, 37–77. Southampton, NY: Parrish Art Museum, 1988.

Bennet, Diane Tarleton, and Linda Tarleton. *W. C. Bryant in Roslyn.* Roslyn, NY: Bryant Library, 1978.

Binse, Harry Lorin. "Rock Hall, an American Manorial Estate." *The Antiquarian,* January 1931.

Bowles, Hamish. "Past Perfect." *Vogue,* August 2009.

Cocks, George William. *History and Genealogy of the Cock-Cocks-Cox Family.* New York: George William Cocks, 1914.

Dean, Arthur W. "Outdoor Life on Long Island." *House & Garden* 19 (March 1911): 212–14.

Dickey, Page. "Anna Wintour's Wild Garden." *T Magazine,* August 8, 2016.

Downs, Joseph. "The Benkard Room." *Metropolitan Museum of Art Bulletin,* January 1948.

E. Belcher Hyde Map Company. *Nassau Estate Map Locust Valley.* New York: E. Belcher Hyde Map Company, 1927. Stony Brook University Map Collection. http://digital.library.stonybrook.edu/.

Eberlein, Harold Donaldson. *Manor Houses and Historic Homes of Long Island and Staten Island.* Philadelphia: J. B. Lippincott, 1928.

"Elinor Latham Williams: Obituary." *Suffolk Times,* January 4, 2018. http://suffolktimes.timesreview.com.

Eyring, Shaun, Kenny Marota, and Richard Guy Wilson, eds. *Re-creating the American Past: Essays on the Colonial Revival.* Charlottesville: University of Virginia Press, 2006.

Flint, Martha Bockée. *Early Long Island: A Colonial Study.* New York: G. P. Putnam's Sons, 1896.

Francis, Joseph Turano. "Two Hundred Years of Family Farm Households, 1700–1900: The Archaeology of the Terry-Mulford Site, Orient (Oysterponds), New York." PhD diss., State University of New York, 1994.

Frazer, Susan Hume. *The Architecture of William Lawrence Bottomley.* New York: Acanthus, 2007.

Fullerton, H. B. "The Small Farm and Its Possibilities on Long Island." *House & Garden* 19 (March 1911): 205–208.

Gabriel, Ralph Henry. *The Evolution of Long Island: A Story of Land and Sea.* New Haven, CT: Yale University Press, 1921.

"Gadfly of the Gold Coast." *Newsday,* January, 30, 1965.

Ganz, Charlotte. *Colonel Rockwell's Scrap-book.* Smithtown, NY: Smithtown Historical Society, 1968.

Gebhard, David. "The American Colonial Revival in the 1930s." *Winterthur Portfolio* 22, nos. 2–3 (Summer–Autumn 1987): 109–148.

Giffen, Edna Davis, Mindy Kronenberg, and Candace Lindemann, eds. *Miller Place.* Chicago: Arcadia, 2010.

Gray, Christopher. "The Unsung Queen of the Colonial Revival." *New York Times,* June 16, 2011.

Griswold, Mac. *The Manor: Three Centuries at a Slave Plantation on Long Island.* New York: Farrar, Straus and Giroux, 2006. pp. 312, 314.

Hall, Louise P. Building Structure Inventory Form: Dicknezer Smith House. Albany: New York Division for Historic Preservation, 1978.

Hammon, Jupiter. "An Evening's Improvement." http://digitalcommons.unl.edu/etas/65.

Hefner, Robert. Building Structure Inventory Form: David Miller House. Albany: New York Division for Historic Preservation, 1983.

Hefner, Robert. "Sylvester Manor: Brinley Sylvester's 1737 House." *Art & Architecture Quarterly East End.* http://www.aaqeastend.com.

Hibbard, Shirley G. *Rock Hall: A Narrative History.* Mineola, NY: Dover, 1997.

"House of William H. Dixon, Esq., St. James, N.Y." *Architectural Forum,* October 1927.

Hunt, Harrison, and Linda Hunt. *William Cullen Bryant's Cedarmere Estate.* Chicago: Arcadia, 2016.

Kornbluth, Jesse. "Living It down in the Un-Hamptons." *Vogue,* August 2009.

Krieg, Joann P, ed. *Long Island Architecture.* Interlaken, NY: Heart of the Lakes, 1991.

Lipman, Andrew. *The Saltwater Frontier: Indians and the Contest for the American Coast.* New Haven, CT: Yale University Press, 2015.

Locust Valley: Long Island. Undated, mid-twentieth-century real-state brochure on Casa Blanca, in the collections of Preservation Long Island.

Lord, Ruth. *Henry F. du Pont and Winterthur: A Daughter's Portrait.* New Haven, CT: Yale University Press, 1999.

MacKay, Robert B., Stanley Lindvall, and Carol Traynor, eds. *AIA Architectural Guide to Nassau and Suffolk Counties, Long Island.* New York: Dover, 1992. pp. 332–44.

Maxwell, William. *A Portrait of William Floyd, Long Islander.* Setauket, NY: Society for the Preservation of Long Island Antiquities, 1956.

McGee, Dorothy Horton. *Raynham Hall, 1738–1960.* Oyster Bay, NY: Town of Oyster Bay, 1961.

McLean, Lydia. "Now I'm Sixty and I Love It." *Vogue,* June 1973.

Merle-Smith, Van S. "Oyster Bay, 1653–1700." MA thesis, Columbia University, 1950.

Murphy, Robert Cushman. *Fish-Shape Paumanok: Nature and Man on Long Island.* Philadelphia: American Philosophical Society, 1964.

National Register of Historic Places, Cock-Cornelius House, Locust Valley, Nassau County, New York, National Register #06000157.

National Register of Historic Places, Hopkins, Samuel House, Miller Place, Suffolk County, New York, National Register #09000057.

National Register of Historic Places, Old Mastic House, Mastic, Suffolk County, New York, National Register #71000066.

National Register of Historic Places, Sylvester Manor, Shelter Island, Suffolk County, New York, National Register #15000178.

National Register of Historic Places, Turbillon, Mill Neck, Nassau County, New York, National Register #11000598.

O'Neale, Sandra A. *Jupiter Hammon and the Biblical Beginnings of African-American Literature.* Metuchen, NJ: Scarecrow, 1993.

Osann, Jean B. *Henry Lloyd's Salt Box Manor House.* Lloyd Harbor, NY: Lloyd Harbor Historical Society, 1982.

Ottusch-Kianka, Donna. Albertson-Meyer, title search report. April 29, 2006.

Raynham Hall Museum. "Architecture." Raynham Hall. Accessed April 2018, https://raynham-hallmuseum.org/.

"The Residence of Wm. H. Dixon, Smithtown, Long Island." *Garden & Home Builder,* May 1927.

Scott, Kenneth, and Susan E. Klaffky. *A History of the Joseph Lloyd Manor House.* Setauket, NY: Society for the Preservation of Long Island Antiquities, 1976.

Smith, Ainsworth. Building Structure Inventory Form: Hopkins Homestead. Albany: New York Division for Historic Preservation, 1976.

Smith, Raymond W. Building Structure Inventory Form: Rock Hall. Albany: New York Division for Historic Preservation, 1976.

Stafford, Sidney Frissell. *Toni Frissell: Photographs, 1933–1967.* New York: Doubleday, 1994.

Starace, Carl A. Building Structure Inventory Form: Sagtikos Manor. Albany: New York Division for Historic Preservation, 1990.

Sterling, Dorothy. *The Outer Islands.* New York: W. W. Norton, 1978.

Stevens, John R. "Restoration of the Powell Farmhouse." *Friends of the Nassau County Historical Museum Bulletin* 4, no. 1 (Spring 1969): 4–11.

Stillinger, Elizabeth. *The Antiquers.* New York: Knopf, 1980.

Studenroth, Zachary. Building Structure Inventory Form: Joseph Lloyd Manor House. Albany: New York Division for Historic Preservation, 1977.

Town of Smithtown. Building Structure Inventory Form: East Farm. Albany: New York Division for Historic Preservation, 1980a.

Town of Smithtown. Building Structure Inventory Form: Thatch Meadow Farm. Albany: New York Division for Historic Preservation, 1980b.

Van Liew, Barbara Ferris. *Long Island Domestic Architecture of the Colonial and Federal Periods.* Setauket, NY: Society for the Preservation of Long Island Antiquities, 1974.

Viemeister, August. *An Architectural Journey through Long Island.* Port Washington, NY: Kennikat, 1974.

Vollmer, William A. "Long Island–Its History and Character." *House & Garden* 19 (March 1911): 202–204.

Wagner, Gay. Building Structure Inventory Form: Cock/Ryan House. Albany: New York Division for Historic Preservation, 1978a.

Wagner, Gay. Building Structure Inventory Form: Stage Coach Inn ("Hay Fever"). Albany: New York Division for Historic Preservation, 1978b.

Whittlesey, C. E. "The Commuter's Long Island." *House & Garden* 19 (March 1911): 209–11.

Williams, Elinor. *The Old House Formerly Terry-Mulford House.* Albany, New York Division for Historic Preservation, 1979.

Woolf, Virginia. "Craftsmanship." BBC audio recording, April 29, 1937. http://www.bbc.com.

Woolsey, Melancthon Lloyd. "The Lloyd Manor of Queens Village." Address delivered at the annual meeting of the New York Branch of the Colonial Lords of Manors in America, New York, April 1923.

Wyckoff, Edith Hay. *The Fabled Past: Tales of Long Island.* Port Washington, NY: Kennikat, 1978.